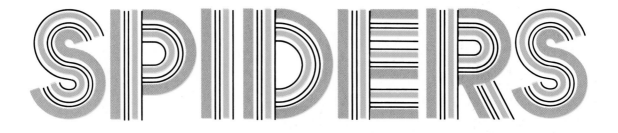

SPIDERS

By Lillian Bason

☐ BOOKS FOR YOUNG EXPLORERS
☐ NATIONAL GEOGRAPHIC SOCIETY

Copyright © 1974 National Geographic Society   Library of Congress Catalog Number 74-10109   Standard Book Number 0-87044-156-6

If you go outdoors
on a summer morning,
you may see the webs
that spiders have made in the night.
You might even look through a magnifying glass
to see the fine silk threads.
And when you look at a web up close,
see if you can find a spider waiting there.

Banded Garden Spider (right)

2

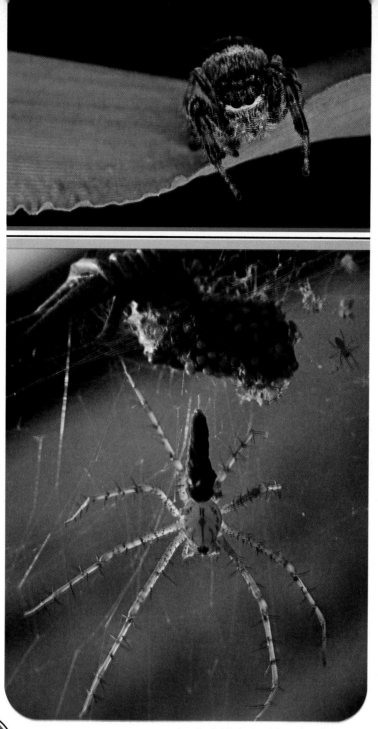

Jumping Spider (top) and Green Lynx Spider

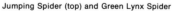

Some spiders build webs. Some do not.
Webs trap grasshoppers
and other insects for spiders to eat.
Some spiders hunt for their food.
They have sharp eyes and speedy legs.
All mother spiders spin soft silk
around their eggs to keep them safe.

4

Black-and-yellow Garden Spider

Fishing Spider

Spiders live in many places.
Some live in holes they dig in the ground.
You can even find spiders in the water.
Others make their homes in the grass.
Have you ever seen a spider
or a spider web in your house?
Spiders live in trees and bushes, too.

Burrowing Wolf Spider

Funnel-web Spider

There are spiders that look like little monsters.
Others have sharp spines and spots.
Some spiders have marks that look like designs.
Spiders can be green, or yellow, or red,
but most are brown, gray, or black.

Spiny-bellied Orb Weaver (top). Orb Weaver (middle). Green Lynx Spider (below)

Jumping Spider

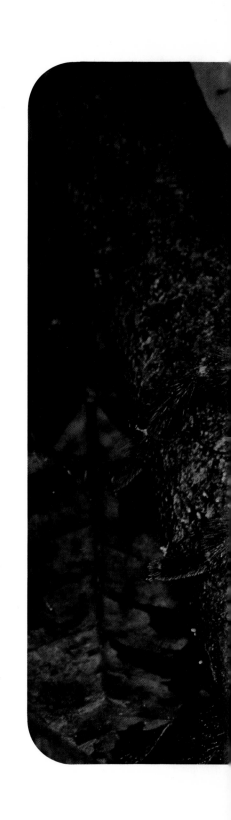

Some spiders are big.
Some spiders are very small.
They can be as small as a fly,
and sometimes they are even smaller.
They can be as tiny as a dot
on a piece of paper.
Some are much bigger.
This garden spider is an inch long.

Tarantula (above) and Garden Spider (left)

The tarantula is the giant of the spider world.
This tarantula can have a body bigger than your fist.
When it stretches its legs out,
it can cover a whole page in this book.

Silver Garden Spider

Wolf Spider

Spiders are not insects.
Insects have six legs, and spiders have eight.
Insects usually have wings. Spiders never do.
Spiders bite with sharp fangs
that carry poison.
Most spiders are not poisonous to people.
But a black widow is a spider to watch out for.
It has a bright red mark on its underside,
and its bite is very poisonous.

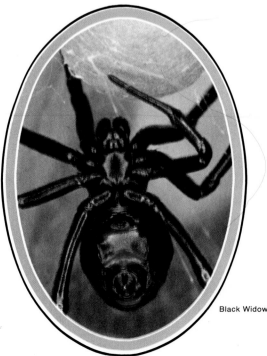

Black Widow

When a spider catches an insect,
it bites it very quickly.
This spider is biting a flower fly.
The black-and-yellow flower fly
looks like a bee.
The spider's bite has a poison
that makes an insect helpless.
It cannot move or get away.
And soon the insect is dead.

Crab Spider

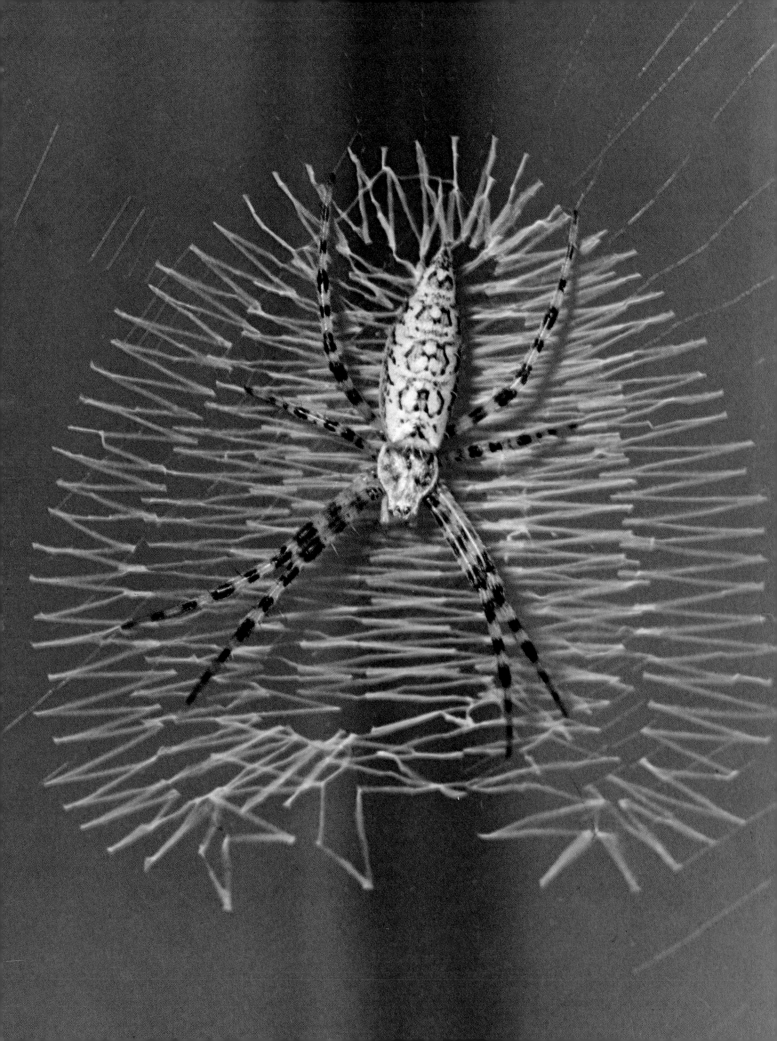

Orb Web

Bowl and Doily Spider Web

piders build webs
in many shapes and sizes.
Some have threads that zigzag
all over the web.
Some webs are round like a circle.
Others look like tents.

Dictyna Web

All spiders spin silk.
The spider makes the silk inside its body.
The thread comes out through tiny holes on its underside.
It can be dry or sticky. Spiders use the sticky thread in the web.
They wrap the dry thread around the insects they catch.

Most spiders also spin a thread as they move around.
This thread, called a dragline, keeps the spider from falling.
It can jump or drop from a tree or bush, and swing safely
on the end of its silk dragline.

Black-and-yellow Garden Spider (top) and Green Lynx Spider

It takes a spider about an hour to spin a web.
When its work is done,
it has made a net of sticky threads.
The thread is thinner than a hair,
but it is very strong.

This spider starts its web
by sending out a thread.
The thread floats in the air
until it sticks to a twig or leaf.

The spider spins more thread
and sticks the thread to other twigs.
Thread also goes
from the center to the sides.

The spider keeps on spinning,
around and around in circles.
Soon its flat, round web is finished.

 wolf spider
doesn't use a web
to get its food.
It comes out of its home
at night,
and races very fast
to catch what it needs to eat.
Here a hungry crab spider waits
for dinner on a pink flower.

Crab Spider and Burrowing Wolf Spider (right)

 trap-door spider spins a silky wall for its home in the ground.

It builds a trapdoor for the roof
by mixing thread and soil together.
Inside, the spider is warm, and dry, and snug.
If an insect walks nearby,
the spider opens the trapdoor and comes out
to catch the insect for dinner.

Water spiders live
in ponds and streams,
and so they catch tiny fish to eat.
A water spider spins its web
on plants that grow underwater.
The spider comes up
to get little bubbles of air.
The air bubbles stick
to the spider's fuzzy legs and body.
The spider takes the air down to its web.
The little bubbles make one big bubble
for an underwater home.

ometimes one spider
will eat another spider.
An enemy like this assassin bug
can catch and eat a spider.
Spiders have many other enemies, too.
Lizards and snakes, toads and birds
also catch spiders whenever they can.

Orb Weaver (above) and Jumping Spider eating Orb Weaver

Black-and-yellow Garden Spider (above) and Large-eyed Jumping Spider

There are millions and millions of busy spiders
in fields and gardens everywhere.
And all summer long
they spin their silky webs.

If you have a garden,
spiders help you because they eat insects
that harm your flowers and plants.

Sometimes a web will break.
But a spider doesn't give up.
It gets back to work and spins another web.
And if you look again another morning,
you may see new webs shining in the sun.

Published by The National Geographic Society
Melvin M. Payne, *President;* Melville Bell Grosvenor, *Editor-in-Chief;*
Gilbert M. Grosvenor, *Editor.*

Prepared by
The Special Publications Division
Robert L. Breeden, *Editor*
Donald J. Crump, *Associate Editor*
Philip B. Silcott, *Senior Editor*
Cynthia Russ Ramsay, *Managing Editor*
Harriet H. Watkins, *Research*

Illustrations
George A. Peterson, *Picture Editor*

Design and Art Direction
Joseph A. Taney, *Staff Art Director*
Josephine B. Bolt, *Associate Art Director*
Ursula Perrin, *Staff Designer*

Production and Printing
Robert W. Messer, *Production Manager*
George V. White, *Assistant Production Manager*
Raja D. Murshed, Nancy W. Glaser, *Production Assistants*
John R. Metcalfe, *Engraving and Printing*
Mary G. Burns, Jane H. Buxton, Marta Isabel Coons, Suzanne J. Jacobson,
  Joan Perry, Marilyn L. Wilbur, *Staff Assistants*

Consultants
Dr. Glenn O. Blough, *Educational Consultant*
Dr. Norman Platnick, *Scientific Consultant, Assistant Curator,*
  Department of Entomology, The American Museum of Natural History
Edith K. Chasnov, Lynn Z. Lang, *Reading Specialists*

Illustrations Credits

James L. Stanfield, *National Geographic Photographer (endsheets, 3);* Richard S. Lee *(1, 14-15);*
Paul A. Zahl, *National Geographic Staff (2, 12-13, 22-23, 24);* Ann Moreton *(4 top, 4-5, 7 bottom,*
8-9, 13 bottom, 17 bottom left, 28, 29, 30-31); James A. and Richard C. Kern *(4 bottom, 19 bottom);*
Larry West *(6-7, 17 top right and bottom right, 32);* James H. Carmichael, Jr. *(7 top, 8 all,*
16, 20-21); John Ballay *(10, 30 top);* Edward S. Ross *(10-11);* Aldo Margiocco *(13 top);*
Harry Ellis *(17 top left);* Richard C. Kern *(18-19);* Janice Healey *(19 top); painting by*
Peter Bianchi *under the direction of arachnologist* John A. L. Cooke © *N.G.S. (21);*
William R. Fonda, *National Geographic Staff (22);* John A. L. Cooke *(24-25);* Robert F. Sisson,
National Geographic Photographer (26, 26-27).

Cover Photograph: Ann Moreton

Wolf Spider